Einstein

The Girl who Hated Maths

HODDER
Wayland

an imprint of Hodder Children's Books

To Anne McNeil and Caroline Sheldon
for supporting and balancing the equation.

To Satoshi Kitamura for visually solving it.

To Kalera for asking in the first place, "Dad, why
can't we migrate to a country where there's no
maths?"

Text copyright © 2002 John Agard
Illustrations copyright © 2002 Satoshi Kitamura

Published in Great Britain in 2002
by Hodder Wayland, an imprint of
Hodder Children's Books

This paperback edition published in 2003 and 2004

The right of John Agard to be identified as the
author of this Work and of Satoshi Kitamura as the
illustrator of this Work has been asserted by them in
accordance with the Copyright, Designs and Patents Act 1988

A catalogue record for this book is available from the British Library

ISBN: 0 7502 42884

Printed and bound in Hong Kong

Hodder Children's Books
A division of Hodder Headline Limited
338 Euston Road, London NW1 3BH

CONTENTS

Einstein
The Girl who Hated Maths

Her parents liked the name
so they called her Einstein.
And how she hated maths.
She'd rather play with cats
or do a drawing of the sunshine.

But they made her count from one to nine
and put one in front of zero.
Ten, they said, would follow.
But it wasn't as much fun
as snowballing in the snow.

So her maths homework never gets done
without a whinge and whine
from that girl Einstein.
She thinks maths is a pain.
Too many numbers nibbling at her brain.

Whoever invented maths
must have been out of their mind.
All those funny little signs
swarming like splodges of ink.
What is Einstein supposed to think?

She didn't really care
that two matching items make a pair
so four pairs of shoes are four times two –
as long as she got to choose
her favourite party-blue.

Two pairs of feet fit four roller skates,
how many pairs of feet fit eight?
'Ah,' sighs Einstein, 'why don't we migrate
to a country where there's no maths.
Tell me and I'll jump on a jet.'

Well, Einstein, wherever you jet-set
– Africa, Europe, India, Tibet –
numbers will greet you on arrival
like letters of the alphabet.
Numbers too are a way of survival.

Yes, wherever you go, maths will follow.
But don't worry, numbers are fine,
her parents would say to their Einstein.
Both were accountants by profession,
though once her dad made a confession.

'Of all the subjects, I must admit
maths was not my favourite.
I was near the bottom of the class.
How do you think I managed to pass?
Ask your mum and she will tell you.'

'Well,' said her mum, 'I've told you before.
Dad was the boy who lived next door.
And I helped him with his maths homework.
Maths, you could say, was our matchmaker
and that was long before calculators.'

It was maths that brought them together.
It was numbers that made their love shine
– they were thirteen at the time –
until one day, six years later,
into the world came cuddly Einstein.

'So,' Einstein said smiling, 'that would mean
I was born when you were nineteen.'
'Right,' said her mum, 'nine times two plus one.'
'Or ten times two less one,' said her dad.
'You see, Einstein, maths isn't that bad.

'Like your two cats, weren't they an addition
to the family?' And Einstein agreed
two cats were two extra mouths to feed.
And her cats soon had six kittens - no lying -
for cats have a way of multiplying.

That meant finding homes for twelve, one by one,
and their going was sad subtraction.
Of course, Einstein got into a mood,
but since cats have nine lives, she knew
her two cats would have nine times two.

'Eighteen,' said Mum, 'that's a lot of lives.'
And she told Einstein a brain-teaser
'Sounds tricky, but nothing's easier.
Now this will test your grasp of digits.
Five cats catch five mice in five minutes.

'How many cats would you need
to catch 100 mice in 100 minutes?
Take your time, Einstein. Don't answer yet,
for it's a question with a catch.
Remember, the mice and minutes match.'

Those same five cats, if they're feeling fit,
would catch 60 mice in 60 minutes
would catch 100 mice in 100 minutes.
The answer was five, Einstein knew it.
And isn't it fun when numbers play tricks?

Without numbers we'd have no address.
The poor postman would be in a mess.
Numbers help us to communicate.
Without them we'd be lost for a birthday date
or how many candles to put on the cake.

Counting began with fingers and toes.
Some even did sums on knuckles and elbows.
Do you know two hands could add up to a billion?
Now we take for granted the gift of zero –
the egg that hatches tens into trillions.

Long, long ago it was the abacus.
Now calculators do our counting for us.
But pebbles, bones, shells and sticks
all played their part in mathematics.
'Numbers,' said her mum and dad, 'make music.'

And sure as flower petals come in fives
like the points of stars in the skies,
Einstein began to feel maths come alive.
And while Mum and Dad clicked their fingers,
Einstein tapped her feet to the beat of numbers.

Keeping Fit

Forget aerobics and gymnastics.
I'm keeping fit with mathematics.
None of this jogging lark
and malarky round the park.

I burn up calories
swivelling my shoulder
three hundred and sixty degrees.
I become a circle
turning on two bent knees.

Now it's doubles and trebles
with toes and knuckles.
I multiply inbreath
by outbreath.
That usually works up a sweat.

Now watch me extend my arms
into parallelograms.
With a twist of the torso
I squat like a zero.
Then to test my flexibility

I stretch and stretch and stretch

                    to infinity.

How Many Is How Many?

How many stars make a sky?
How many waves make a sea?

How many sands make a beach?
How many leaves make a tree?

How many trees make a forest?
How many drops make a rainfall?

Whatever number you guess
will always seem kind of small,

for a billion sounds like a lot
to the ears of an earthling,

but to galaxies spiralling
a billion is only a dot.

.100000

Depending
on its spot
it can lessen
what you've got.

It reduces
the highest
number
to rock-bottom.

Can make even
a million
seem less
than a lot.

All power
to the dot.
the dot.
the dot.

The Day the Numbers Spoke

Number one said:
Where I'm going, I go alone.
That is me, myself and I.

Number two said:
I'm part of a perfect couple
and we're heading for the sky.

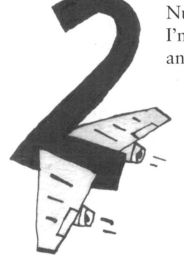

Number three said:
I've had enough of triangles
O to be a circle for a while.

Number four said:
North, South, East, West, I'm all about,
At home in every direction.

Number five said:
Simply gaze at a single star
and I'll twinkle my reflection.

Number six said:
My fortune takes me far and wide
for I'm the top throw on the dice.

Number seven said:
To the heavens that's where I'll go.
Look no higher than a rainbow.

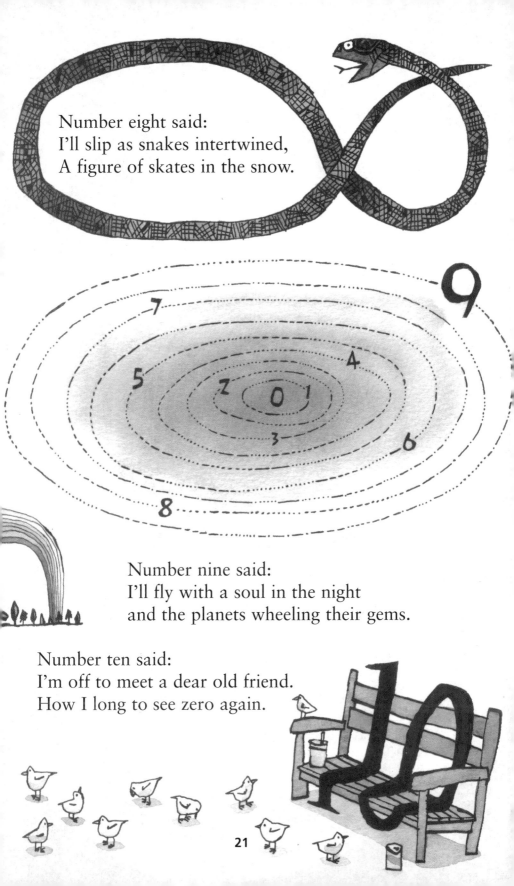

Number eight said:
I'll slip as snakes intertwined,
A figure of skates in the snow.

Number nine said:
I'll fly with a soul in the night
and the planets wheeling their gems.

Number ten said:
I'm off to meet a dear old friend.
How I long to see zero again.

0

Zero
you mischievous
goblin nought
that can make
a number grow

into hundreds
into thousands
into millions
into billions
into trillions
into zillions

and on
and on
into a forever
horizon
where a glimpse is caught
of naughty nought
rolling like an egg
that's pleased with itself
because little nought knows
that multiplied by zero
the biggest zillion
returns to
zero.

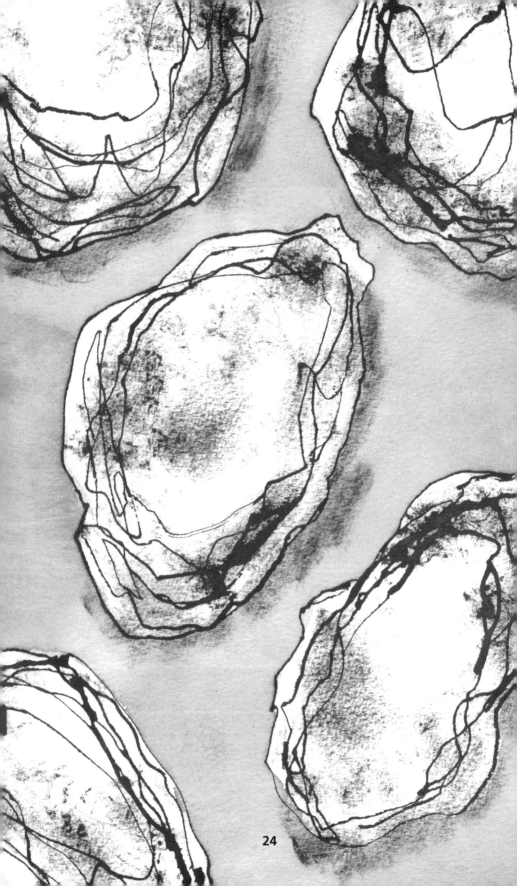

24

Oyster Girl

They call me Oyster Girl
And I'm at home in sea world.

I skip among coral.
I hopscotch on seaweed.
Under a moon that's full
I play You-Follow-I-Lead.

Remember, all you who stand
and gaze at the sea,
Oysters there are many
but in every thousand

You'll find only one pearl
And that's me, Oyster Girl.

A Wonderful 100 Per Cent

Since my body
is 70 per cent water,
same as planet earth,
it's no wonder
when I cry
and when I laugh
streams flow from my eyes,
and when I do a wee
I become a little fountain,
and when I perspire
I'm all river
and every vein
a running tributary.

But what of the other
30 per cent of me?
O my bones are minerals,
my teeth undiscovered gems.
Let me just say in all modesty,
I'm a wonderful 100 per cent.

The Mental Arithmetic Twist

It's a new dance groove, goes like this,
it's the Mental Arithmetic Twist.

Twist your brain cells round addition,
tune in to the plus–plus rhythm.

You don't need a calculator
to be a counting operator.

What's a million but one and six zeroes,
and you've got ten fingers and ten toes.

And since a million's ten to the power of six,
you can snap and tap and shake your hips.

Yeah do the Mental Arithmetic Twist.
Can you dig it? Can you jig it?

An Ark, An Ark

An Ark, an Ark,
Noah shall make
for when the skies shall grow dark
and the thunder shall shake.

Three hundred cubits
of length he shall give it.
Fifty cubits
of width he shall give it.
Thirty cubits
of height he shall give it.

Better start building quick.
But Brother Noah is losing his wits.
The poor man no good at arithmetic.

Ishango Bone

Ishango Bone
how old are you
and what did you do
and where were you from
before this museum?
I've so many questions.
Ishango Bone
are you really
8000 years old? Who knows?
And was your home
a lake that flows
into the River Nile
high in the mountains
of Central Africa?

Ishango Bone
before you became
an object to be gazed at,
did those notches
row by row
help the Ishango
to add and subtract
and mark the phases
of the moon?

Ishango Bone,
one last question.
This calculator
that helps me with my maths –
will it like you
become an artefact?

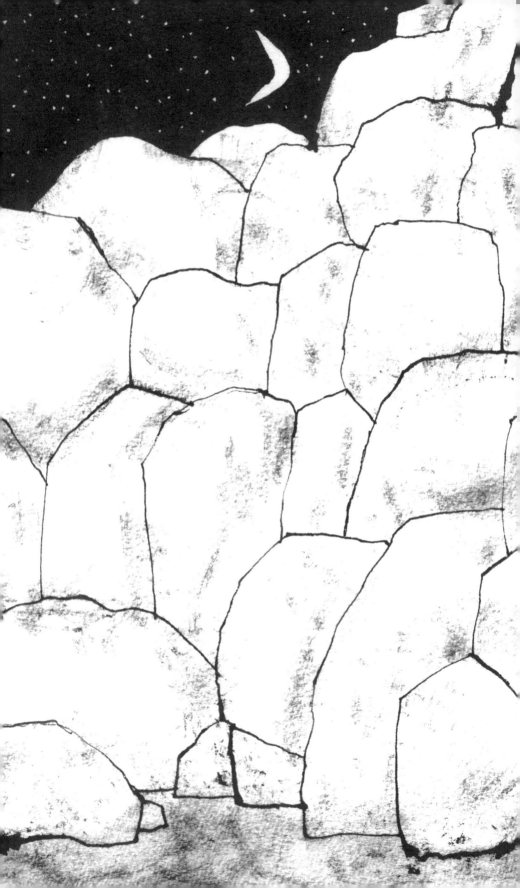

Who Will Grieve for Forty Thieves

Forty thieves
Forty thieves
O who will grieve
for forty thieves?

Not I said Ali Baba
You'll have to look far to find badder.

Not I said the judge
The scales of justice will not budge.

Not I said the rich man
They stole my gold and away they ran.

Forty thieves
Forty thieves
O who will grieve
for forty thieves?

I will said a voice from a cave
I will grieve for forty thieves.
I who open at Open Sesame
grieve for all who enter eternity.

Day Keeper

Day keeper
Day keeper
Where do you keep days?

Do you dissolve them in rivers of sleep?
Do you scatter them for the winds to reap?

Day keeper
Day keeper
Where do you keep days?

Three hundred and sixty-five gathered
each year, plus an extra leap one
every four years. Where are they? All gone
the way of all days.

Back to tomorrow
which will soon be yesterday
even as we speak today.

Day keeper
Day keeper
Answer me.

Is there no bottom
to your bag of memory?

The Polygons

Polly Polygon
and Peter Polygon
lived all their lives
bounded by straight lines.

And down at the club
of curves and squiggles,
members had a giggle
at the straight-lined couple,
for polygons weren't welcome.

'O, can't be much fun
being a polygon,
how we'd hate to be straight.'

'On the contrary,'
said Mr and Mrs Polygon.
'We haven't a single complaint.

'For we party with pentagons,
hobnob with hexagons
and spend quality time
with quadrilaterals.
We're party animals.

'And once in moonlit Havana
we danced the rhombus
to sounds of the rhumba.
All our lives we've been straight
and we've managed quite well
without any curves and bends.

'Mind you,' said the Polygons,
'We do have a wide circle of friends.'

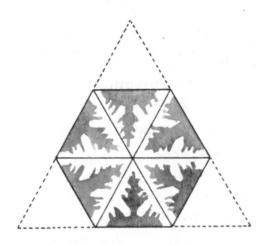

Once Upon An Equilateral Triangle

An equilateral triangle
grew tired of being equilateral.
No, I want to live life to the full.
It's all right having sixty degrees
in every pocket of my angles,
but I'd rather take off in a breeze,
footloose as a bird or a bee.
I wonder if I can wangle
myself into some new form or shape.
So the equilateral triangle
divided each of its sides into thirds
and did a little whirl and a swirl.
It was geometry in motion.
Suddenly, something special occurred.
With a final spin and a shake,
the triangle changed to a hexagon,
taking the form of, guess what? A snowflake.

On Cloud Nine

On cloud nine
everything's fine

nothing's ever
at sixes and sevens

on cloud nine
all is heaven.

Everybody goes about
in Sunday best

people are dressed
to the nines

on cloud nine
everywhere is a song

and one gets along with one.

Quipu Chant

By coloured knots on strings,
we Keepers of the Knots
we remember
our Inca beginnings.

By the Quipu, our calendar.
By the Quipu, our ledger.
By the Quipu, our message-bearer.

By the counting threads
of the Quipu,
we Keepers of the Knots
we account for
the ears of corn
the heads of cattle
the gold of the sun
the silver of the moon
the roaming llama.

By the living threads
of the Quipu,
we Keepers of the Knots
we account for
the fallen in battle,
the numbers gone to Pachacamac
god of earth and time,
and the numbers still here
to breathe rain's miracle.

By the talking threads
of the Quipu,
we Keepers of the Knots
we keep the past un-dead.
We who unravel
the Quipu's secrets
as the hours unravel us.
We Keepers of the Knots.
Let it not be said
that we forgot.

Triskaidekaphobia

TRISKAIDEKAPHOBIA? What does it mean?
It's when someone's scared of number 13.
But how can a number be scary?
Don't ask me, ask the dictionary.

Archimedes' Mother Speaks to the Press

I knew he'd follow
a mathematical path.
Don't ask how. Mums just know.
Besides, he always spent
such a long time in the bath,
tracing spirals and segments
on his olive-oiled skin.

It became a family joke –
the way he would toy with the soap,
calculating its volume,
testing its equilibrium.
You could say I was a patient Mum.
By the time he'd stepped from the bath,
he was glistening
with parabolas,
or so he called them.
I just knew when I heard the news
of someone running stark naked
through the streets of Syracuse –
some mathematician
according to rumour –

I just knew it could only be
my Archie,
my bath-loving doodler,
running in the altogether,
inviting the world to join him
in his EUREKA, EUREKA.

The Soul from Different Angles

The soul is a spiral,
said the first mathematician.
A shell awakening from sleep.

The soul is a straight line,
said the second mathematician.
An arrow that pierces deep.

The soul is a triangle,
said the third mathematician.
The unity of three in one.

The soul is a square,
said the fourth mathematician.
Each side a benediction.

The soul is a circle,
said the fifth mathematician.
A wheel forever turning.

How shall I put it?
said the last mathematician,
The soul is anybody's guess.

But I'd like to suggest
the soul is an egg
holding itself within itself.

You Isosceles

Please.
I didn't mean to be rude
when I called you Isosceles.
It's not some kind of disease.
Honest.
Just the way your trousers dangle
with your legs apart –
reminds me of a triangle
with two sides of equal length
and your shoes
two equal angles
that could do with a shining.
Never mind my shoes,
You Hypothenuse.

ImproperFractions

Just because our numerator
is bigger than
our denominator
is no excuse
for calling us
improper.
Don't make us laugh!
Let $^{15}/_2$
be rewritten
as $7\,^1/_2$.
This gives a fraction
great satisfaction
and we like to think
it's a proper
transaction.

Bisector

They call me Bisector.
That's what I do best. Bisect.
And I'm no respecter
of angle or line.
I'll bisect them any time.
Bisecting is my line.

They call me Bisector.
The mean mediator.
The perky perpendicular.
I may sound like a bully
but deep down I'm a softie.
I believe in equality.

So I bisect an angle
into equal parts, only fair,
and each one gets an equal share.
I bisect right, I bisect left,
I even bisect myself.
That's, of course, my greatest test.

Number 9 Would Like A Word

Take any number.
Multiply by 9.
The answer combined
will add up to 9.
O isn't it divine
to be number 9?

The number of stitches
that could be saved
by a stitch in time.
The number of twists
to Hell's river Styx.
The number of steps
to Heaven's City.

The number of branches
on the cosmic tree.
The number of Muses
to give inspiration.
The number of heads
on a Chinese dragon.
The number of months
for a baby to arrive.
The number of lives
permitted a cat.
And I'll tell you what,
I Number 9
feel even more divine
when dressed up to the nines.

A Beeline as the Crow Flies

How do you travel
the shortest distance
between two points?
Would you do a zig-zag prance?

The bee knows but says nothing.
Just makes a honeybeeline
from flower to flower
in a dance of nectar.

The crow knows but says nothing.
Just joins earth to sky
in an embrace of near and far.
As the crow flies, as the crow flies.

I know.
Just make a beeline for the fridge
where the ice-cream's cool,
then fly like a crow to my room.

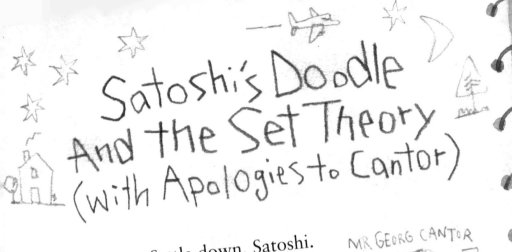

Satoshi's Doodle And the Set Theory (with Apologies to Cantor)

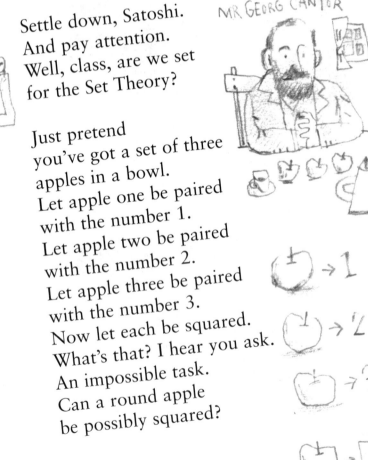

MR GEORG CANTOR

MR A GARD

Settle down, Satoshi.
And pay attention.
Well, class, are we set
for the Set Theory?

Just pretend
you've got a set of three
apples in a bowl.
Let apple one be paired
with the number 1.
Let apple two be paired
with the number 2.
Let apple three be paired
with the number 3.
Now let each be squared.
What's that? I hear you ask.
An impossible task.
Can a round apple
be possibly squared?

Oh yes, down to the core,
as two times two make four,
for a number squared
is that by itself multiplied
as three times three make nine
and nine times nine – eighty-one.
We can go on and on and on
and yet,
and yet no nearer, a glimpse
of that number beyond the beyond.

Let me put it like this.
Since one apple holds
all the appleness
of a set in a bowl –
which is a little universe –
then an apple forever squared
multiplies its appleness
more times than can be told,
as your doodle, Satoshi,
simply by being forever squared
can multiply its doodleness
into a galaxy
of never-ending doodles.

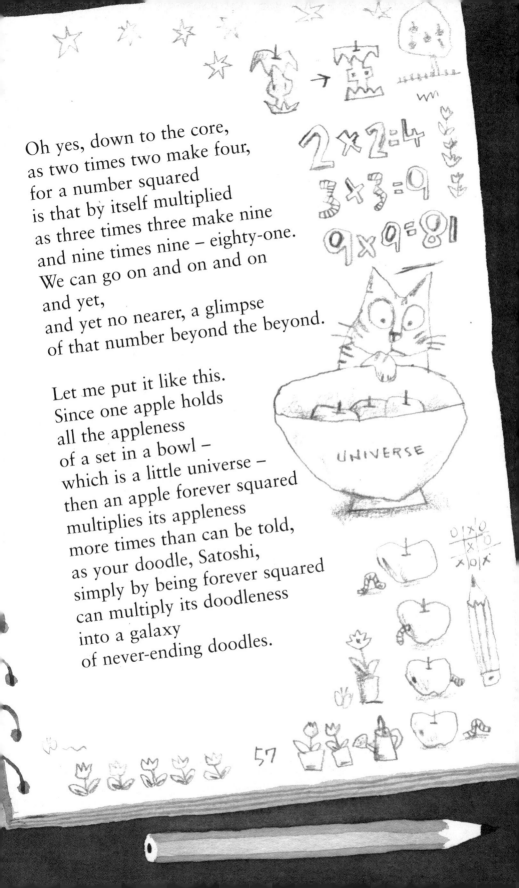

$$2 \times 2 = 4$$
$$3 \times 3 = 9$$
$$9 \times 9 = 81$$

UNIVERSE

But enough of the Set Theory.
Tomorrow we do sub-sets,
which are sets within sets.
Meanwile, here's a tongue-twister
to tease your mind-sets.

Henny Penny, the setting hen,
on a nest of three eggs squared three times round.
How many eggs in the setting sun
Did Henny Penny actually sit upon?

Animal Arithmetic

What's a herd of cows
to a cow?

What's a flock of sheep
to a sheep?

What's a pack of wolves
to a wolf?

What's a gang of geese
to a goose?

Animals, they say, are no good
at arithmetic?

Mother Hen doesn't agree –
scurrying from her nest
stirring up a fuss
scratching the dust
for that one minus

her missing egg.

The Weight of Words

Diplodocus
weighed 11 tons.

Brontosaurus
weighed 30 tons.

Brachiosaurus
weighed 100 tons.

Tyrannosaurus
the fiercest of all
weighed only 6 1/2 tons.

Where are they now
these terribly spectacular lizards?

O if only they had known
the weight of words
in my Roget's Thesaurus,
which doesn't weigh much,

they might have told their own
story for us.

A Mountain of a Heart

We elephants have a heart
that weighs 48 pounds –
more than 20 kilograms.
A mountain of a beast
deserves a mountain of a heart.

And when we hug trunk-to-trunk,
it's a larger than life cuddle.
And when two elephants bask
in the goodness of water splashed,
our grey flanks shine with knowing

that a heart weighs as much as love lets it.

No Bananas Among No Monkeys

Three bananas among three monkeys.
How many does each monkey receive?

One.

A thousand bananas among a thousand monkeys.
How many does each monkey receive?

One.

But there at the back of the class
one little boy raised a finger
with a burning question to ask.

'What if no bananas
were divided among no monkeys?'

The whole class found it funny.
They thought, it's only Ramanujan –
for this was the boy's name –
being a mischievous Hanuman
with another one of his games.

But from the teacher's expression
it was a serious question
that young Ramanujan had proposed.

'Well done, Ramanujan,
you've taken us far beyond
the world of zeros.
No bananas among no monkeys
has baffled maths minds for centuries.'

Fermat Expostulates His Last Margin to an Intruder

Don't you know you should knock
before entering?

You can't just barge in
while I'm working in the margin.

It's a sign of good gumption
to propose an assumption

and leave others to imagine
and ponder the proof.

So I'll scribble in the margin
$X^n + Y^n = Z^n$.

That should keep them guessing.
Yes, I'll have them all goofed.

Just between you and me,
of course the margin's wide enough

for sums of squares and cubes
and to prove what's what of my theory.

So in my grave I'll have the last laugh.
Here lies Fermat who lied

to keep the margin marvellous.

Recipe for a Magic Square

A yellow river.

A Chinese emperor.

A turtle's back.

Odd

Two odd numbers
always add up
to an even.

But two even numbers
never add up
to an odd.

We odd numbers
like to think we're
the handiwork of God.

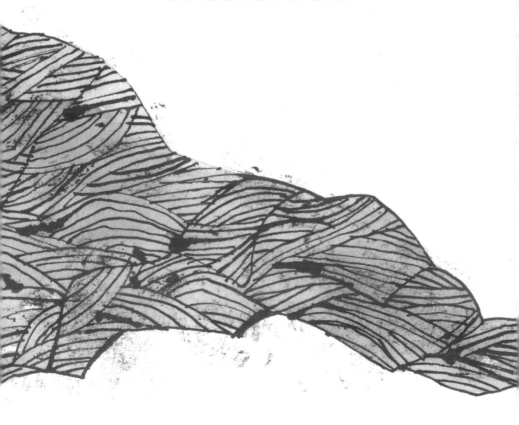

Anyone For Pi?

Pie in the sky.
Pie in the face.
Both bring a smile
to the human race.

But the pie that fills
with most wonder of all
is the pie they serve
at the mathematicians' ball

for their *pi* has no *e*
– it's no ordinary pastry –
and they sit in circles
of opulence

as they feast on diameter
and circumference.

'It's the ratio that matters,'
they conclude with a sigh
as they raise their glasses to *pi*.
'Come hell, come heaven,
let's propose a toast
to twenty-two over seven.'

A Parallel Meeting

On a day of unparalleled sunshine,
two strangers walk on parallel lines.
And parallel lines, they say, never meet.

But when sun pours down its honey-sweet
glow to make hearts glad for a summer,
two parallel 'hellos' find each other.

The Coming of the Hedrons

Tetrahedron
was a giant
with four equilateral faces,
so he stood out in a crowd
of folks with only one face.
Let's just say he was different,
until one day Tetrahedron
met a certain lady giant
named Octahedron
who had twice as many faces.
It was solid love at first sight,
for they had much in common.
They'd gaze at each other spellbound
and nuzzle faces with mighty sighs
and beautiful was the sound
of their names on each other's tongues.
O Tetrahedron
O Octahedron
Why don't we combine forms
to produce multiple hedrons?

And so a new generation
of multi-faced giants
began to walk the earth.

Hexahedron
of the six faces,
Dodecahedron
of the twelve faces,
Icosahedron
of the twenty faces.

How the folks with only one face
looked on in ancient wonder
at their geometric radiance.

Gone, gone are the dragons,
fallen to our weapons.
What's to be done with these hedrons?
Shall we approach them with a sword
or shall we join their cosmic dance?

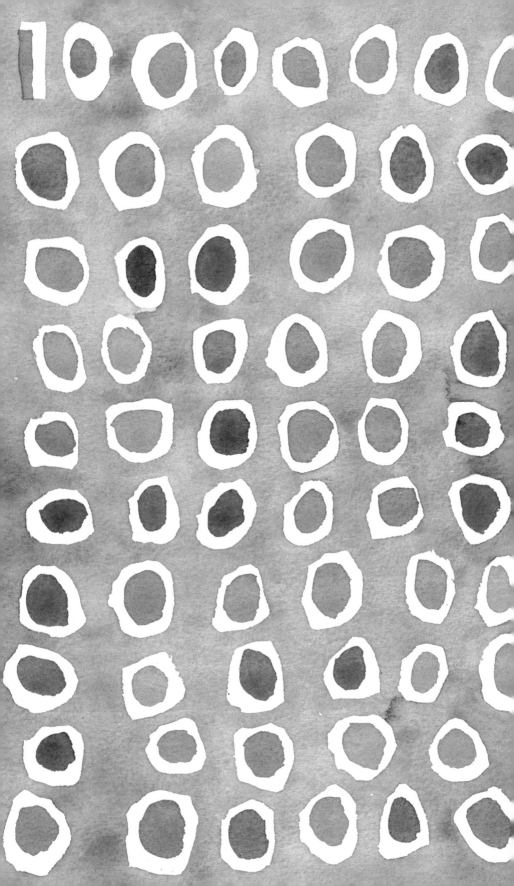

I am Googol

I am Googol
the goggle-eyed One,
leader of 100 zeros.

So gather your army
of trillions and quintillions.
I will outnumber their atoms.
For when I Googol
multiply myself
googol by googol,
let all the minds of East and West
be prepared to be googolplexed.

Not Half Scared

If a quarter moon
is one fourth of a full moon,

and if a fifth of a star
is one twinkling point,

and if I leave my door ajar
which is to say half-open
(or should that be half-closed?)
on a Halloween night,

and if half a pumpkin
comes creeping up the stairs
would I be a fraction scared?

Not half.

Sharing the Same Equation

Did Einstein, my namesake,
have a cat to sit on his lap
when he pondered gravitation?
No reason why a mathematician and a cat
can't share the same equation.

I wonder what his cat would make
of $E = mc^2$ and stuff like that?
Sure, a cat to a mathematician
is much more than a puss.
I'd say it was a plus,
for cats they say walk in straight lines
and are known to be passionately curious.
'And all I have,' said Einstein, 'is my curiosity.'

But I have my own theory.
Behind the whiskers of his moustache,
brainy Einstein was a cat in disguise
longing to ride on a beam of light
and paw at the laws of gravity.

Notes

p.30 Ishango Bone: Excavated in Africa and thought to be the oldest mathematical object, this fossilised baboon bone dates back more than 8,000 years. Some say its notches formed a counting device and might also have been used by African women for counting the phases of the moon. The Ishango Bone is now housed in the Institute for Natural Sciences in Brussels.

p.40 Quipu: Though the Incas had no written language, they used the quipu (meaning knot) for keeping records and accounts. Knots on cords of different colours became a filing system.

p.44 Archimedes was concerned with finding out how much weight a body loses when submerged in water. During one of his legendary baths more than 2,000 years ago, the story goes he found the answer and ran naked through the streets of Syracuse in Sicily shouting "Eureka! Eureka!" ("I found it! I found it!")

p.56 German mathematician Georg Cantor (1845-1918) explored levels of infinity based on a theory of "sets and sub-sets." In case anyone finds this theory unsettling, remember Cantor said, "My theory is solid. I have drawn its principles from the first cause of all created things."

p.62 Indian mathematician Srinivasa Ramanujan (1887-1920) taught himself mathematics by borrowing books from the library. He performed his calculations on a slate and left behind hundreds of intriguing formulas in notebooks. For Ramanujan, "the universe is a product of zero and infinity."

p.64 Seventeenth-century French mathematician Pierre de Fermat wrote in his copy of *Arithmetica*, "I have found a truly marvellous proof which this margin is too narrow to contain." This proof for a certain equation was to keep the best mathematical minds busy for more than 350 years. Andrew Wiles, a Cambridge-born mathematician, is credited with solving this puzzle, famously known as "Fermat's Last Theorem".

p.66 The Magic Square contains numbers arranged in such a way that whether you add from left to right or right to left, up down, or diagonally, the total is always the same. According to one Chinese legend, the Magic Square was revealed to the Emperor Yu through the markings on the back of a magic turtle.

p.75 Googol is the number one followed by a hundred zeros (or ten to the hundredth power). According to mathematical legend, American mathematician Dr Edward Kasner was given the word by his young nephew.

p.78 Nobel-prize winning German-American physicist and mathematician Albert Einstein (1879-1955) also played the violin, which he said helped him with his theory of relativity. One of his teachers described the young Einstein as "stupid." The older Einstein once said, "Do not worry about your difficulties in mathematics, I can assure you that mine are still greater."

Since it took me three attempts to pass my O-level maths, I would have been completely googolplexed without the help of a number of books. Among those I'm grateful to are
The Universal History of Numbers From Prehistory To The Invention Of The Computer by Georges Ifrah, translated from the French by David Bellos, E.F. Harding, Sophie Wood, and Ian Mark (Harvill Press 1998)
The Magic Of Mathematics by Theoni Pappas
(Wide World Publishing/Tetra1994)
The Mystery Of Numbers by Annemarie Schimmel
(Oxford University Press 1993)
The Man Who Loved Only Numbers by Paul Hoffman (Fourth Estate 1998)
Numbers The Universal Language by Denis Guedj (Gallimard 1996),
English translation by Lory Frankel (Harry H. Abrams 1997)
Fermat's Last Theorem – Unlocking the Secret of an Ancient Mathematical Problem by Amir D Aczel (Four Walls Eight Windows 1996)
The story Of Numbers – How Mathematics Has Shaped Civilisation by John McLeish (Fawcett Columbine 1991)
The Crest Of the Peacock – Non-European Roots Of Mathematics by George Gheverghese Joseph (Penguin Books 1992)
Zero – The Biography Of A Dangerous Idea by Charles Seife
(Souvenir Press 2000)
And to Satoshi's mind-teasing e-mails.